wraps
FOR ALL SEASONS™

Shawls and wraps can take any outfit from ho-hum to fabulous! Designer Andee Graves has created such an outstanding collection of wraps that you won't know which one to make first. She has included shawls perfect for every climate and season. The six designs cover a broad range of shapes from square, round, triangular, moebius wrap and a ruana—certainly something for everyone! Whether making these as gifts or for yourself, you will fall in love with the beauty of each unique design.

Summer Seaside Shawl *page 7*

Autumn Days Shawlette, *page 10*

Table of Contents

Hint of Spring

Skill Level
 ◼◼◻◻ EASY

Finished Measurements
40½ inches wide across shoulders x 17 inches long from shoulders to bottom edge

Materials
- Berroco Vintage Colors medium (worsted) weight acrylic/wool/nylon yarn (3½ oz/217 yds/100g per hank):
    3 hanks #5222 oasis
- Berroco Vintage medium (worsted) weight acrylic/wool/nylon yarn (3½ oz/217 yds/100g per hank):
    2 hanks # 5183 lilacs
- Size I/9/5.5mm crochet hook or size needed to obtain gauge
- Tapestry needle
- Stitch markers

Gauge
In pattern: 7 sc and 6 ch-2 sps = 4 inches; 16 rows = 4 inches

Take time to check gauge.

Pattern Notes
This shawl is worked from the top down with increases at each end and at the 2 corner points. To make it easier to find where to work last stitch in each row of mesh pattern, place stitch marker in 2nd chain of beginning chain-4.

Weave in ends as work progresses.

Chain-4 at beginning of row counts as first half double crochet and chain-2 unless otherwise stated.

Join with slip stitch as indicated unless otherwise stated.

Chain-3 at beginning of row does not count as a stitch unless otherwise stated.

Special Stitches
First foundation single crochet (first foundation sc): Ch 2, insert hook in 2nd ch from hook, yo, pull up lp, yo, pull through 1 lp on hook (*see illustration A—ch-1 completed*), yo, pull through both lps on hook (*see illustrations B and C—sc completed*).

Next foundation single crochet (next foundation sc): [Insert hook in last ch-1 made (*see illustration A*), yo, pull up lp, yo, pull through 1 lp on hook (*see illustration B—ch-1 completed*), yo, pull through both lps on hook (*see illustrations C and D—sc completed*)] as indicated.

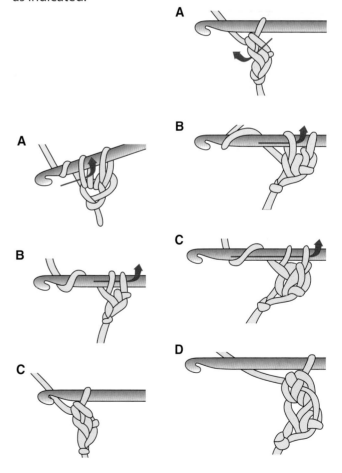

First Foundation Single Crochet   **Next Foundation Single Crochet**

Half shell: ([Dc, ch 1] twice, dc) in indicated sp.

Shell: ([Dc, ch 1] 3 times, dc) in indicated sp.

Large shell: ([Dc, ch 1] 5 times, dc) in indicated sp.

Point shell: (Dc, ch 1, [tr, ch 1] twice, dc) in indicated sp.

Shawl

Body

Row 1: With oasis, **first foundation sc** *(see Special Stitches)*, 12 **next foundation sc** *(see Special Stitches)*, **ch 4** *(see Pattern Notes)*, working on opposite side of foundation sc, (sc, ch 2, sc) in first st, [ch 2, sk next st, sc in next st] 5 times, ch 2, sk next st, (sc, ch 2, sc, ch 2, hdc) in last st, place marker in 2nd and 9th ch-2 sps, turn. *(2 hdc, 9 sc, 10 ch-2 sps)*

Row 2: Ch 4, sc in next ch-2 sp, ch 2, sk next st, (sc, ch 2, sc) in marked sp, move marker to ch-2 sp just made, [ch 2, sk next st, sc in next ch-2 sp] 6 times, ch 2, sk next st, (sc, ch 2, sc) in marked sp, move marker to ch-2 sp just made, ch 2, sk next st, sc in next ch-2 sp, ch 2, hdc in 2nd ch of beg ch-4, turn. *(2 hdc, 12 sc, 13 ch-2 sps)*

Row 3: Ch 4, sc in next ch-2 sp, *[ch 2, sc in next ch-2 sp] across to marked ch-2 sp, ch 2, (sc, ch 2, sc) in marked sp, move marker to ch-2 sp just made, rep from * once, [ch 2, sc in next ch-2 sp] across to last ch-2 sp, ch 2, hdc in 2nd ch of beg ch-4, turn. *(2 hdc, 15 sc, 16 ch-2 sps)*

Rows 4–55: Rep row 3. At end of last row, fasten off. *(2 hdc, 171 sc, 172 ch-2 sps)*

Border

Row 1: Hold Body with RS facing and row 55 at top, **join** *(see Pattern Notes)* lilacs in end of row 55 of body, ch 4, sc in next ch-2 sp, *[ch 2, sc in next ch-2 sp] across to marked ch-2 sp, ch 2, (sc, ch 2, sc) in marked sp, move marker to ch-2 sp just made, rep from * once, [ch 2, sc in next ch-2 sp] across to last ch-2 sp, ch 2, hdc in 2nd ch of beg ch-4, turn. *(2 hdc, 174 sc, 175 ch-2 sps)*

Row 2: Rep row 3. *(2 hdc, 177 sc, 178 ch-2 sps)*

Row 3: Ch 3 *(see Pattern Notes)*, dc in first st, **half shell** *(see Special Stitches)* in next ch-2 sp, *sk next sc, sc in next st, sk next sc**, **shell** *(see Special Stitches)* in next ch-2 sp, rep from * 18 times, ending last rep at **, **large shell** *(see Special Stitches)* in marked ch-2 sp, move stitch marker to 3rd ch-1 sp of large shell, [sk next sc, sc in next st, sk next sc, shell in next ch-2 sp] 20 times, large shell in marked ch-2 sp, move stitch marker to 3rd ch-1 sp of large shell, [sk next sc, sc in next st, sk next sc, shell in next ch-2 sp] 18 times, sk next sc, sc in next st, sk next st, half shell in last ch-2 sp, dc in 2nd ch of beg ch-4, turn. *(2 large shells, 56 shells, 2 half shells, 2 dc, 59 sc)*

Row 4: Ch 3, 2 dc in first st, (2 tr, ch 1, dc) in next st, ch 1, hdc next ch-1 sp, *ch 1, sk next st, sc in next ch-1 sp, ch 1, sk next 3 sts, sc in next ch-1 sp, ch 1, sk next st**, **point shell** *(see Special Stitches)* in next ch-1 sp, rep from * 18 times, ending last rep at **, hdc in next ch-1 sp, ch 1, sk next st, point shell in marked ch-1 sp, ch 1, sk next st, hdc next ch-1 sp, [ch 1, sk next st, sc in next ch-1 sp, ch 1, sk next 3 sts, sc in next ch-1 sp, ch 1, sk next st, point shell in next ch-1 sp] 20 times, ch 1, sk next st, sc in next ch-1 sp, ch 1, sk next 3 sts, sc in next ch-1 sp, ch 1, sk next st, hdc in next ch-1 sp, ch 1, sk next st, point shell in marked ch-1 sp, ch 1, sk next st, hdc next ch-1 sp, [ch 1, sk next st, sc in next ch-1 sp, ch 1, sk next 3 sts, sc in next ch-1 sp, ch 1, sk next st, point shell in next ch-1 sp] 18 times, ch 1, sk next st, sc in next ch-1 sp, ch 1, sk next 3 sts, sc in next ch-1 sp, ch 1, sk next st, hdc in next st, ch 1, (dc, ch 1, 2 tr) next st, 2 dc last st. Do not turn. *(58 point shells, 4 tr, 6 dc, 6 hdc, 116 sc, 183 ch-1 sps)*

Edging

Rnd 1: Now working in rnds, , working across next side in ends of rows, ch 1, sc in end of row 4, ch 2, sl st in top of last st of row 3, ch 1, sc in ch-3 sp at end of row 2, ch 2, sl st in top of last st of row 2, 2 sc in end of row 2, 2 sc in end of each of next 55 rows, sc in end of next row, **sc dec** *(see Stitch Guide)* in end of same row and first st of foundation row, sc in each of

Continued on page 12

Sassy Spring Wrap

Skill Level

◼◼◼◻ **INTERMEDIATE**

Finished Measurements

16½ inches wide x 42 inches in circumference

Materials

- Plymouth Yarn Encore Mega super bulky (super chunky) weight acrylic/wool yarn (3½ oz/64 yds/100g per ball): 5 balls #0137 California pink
- Size O/12mm hook or size needed to obtain gauge
- Tapestry needle

6 SUPER BULKY

Gauge

In pattern: 9 foundation sc = 4 inches; 4 rows = 4 inches

Take time to check gauge.

Pattern Notes

Wrap is worked on a row of foundation single crochet that is twisted 180 degrees and joined. Round 1 is worked in both top and bottom of the foundation row stitches.

For a longer wrap, increase the number of foundation single crochets in groups of 9 stitches.

Weave in ends as work progresses.

Join with slip stitch as indicated unless otherwise stated.

Chain-4 at beginning of round counts as first double crochet and chain-1 unless otherwise stated.

Special Stitches

First foundation single crochet (first foundation sc): Ch 2, insert hook in 2nd ch from hook, yo, pull up lp, yo, pull through 1 lp on hook *(see illustration A— ch-1 completed)*, yo, pull through both lps on hook *(see illustrations B and C—sc completed).*

Next foundation single crochet (next foundation sc): [Insert hook in last ch-1 made *(see illustration A)*, yo, pull up lp, yo, pull through 1 lp on hook *(see illustration B—ch-1 completed)*, yo, pull through both lps on hook *(see illustrations C and D—sc completed)*] as indicated.

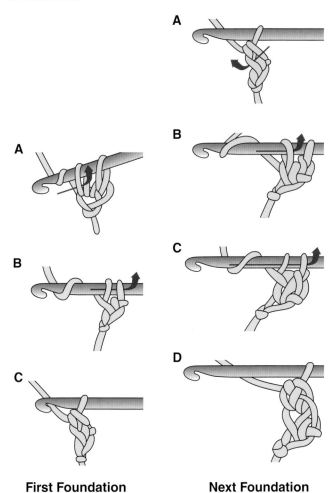

First Foundation Single Crochet

Next Foundation Single Crochet

Fan: ([Dc, ch 1] 5 times, dc) in indicated place.

Shell: (2 dc, ch 3, 2 dc) in indicated place.

Wrap

Foundation rnd: First foundation sc *(see Special Stitches)*, 89 **next foundation sc** *(see Special Stitches)*, twist foundation row 180 degrees, **join** *(see Pattern Notes)* in bottom of first foundation sc. *(90 foundation sc)*

Continued on page 18

Summer Seaside Shawl

Skill Level

 EASY

Finished Measurements

80 inches wide across top edge x 38 inches long from top to bottom point

Materials

- Universal Yarn Bamboo Pop light (DK) weight cotton/bamboo yarn (3½ oz/292 yds/100g per ball):
    3 balls #205 brilliant blues
    2 balls #106 turquoise
- Size H/8/5mm crochet hook or size needed to obtain gauge
- Tapestry needle
- Stitch markers

Gauge

In pattern: 8 sc and 7 ch-2 sps = 4 inches; 18 rows = 4 inches

Take time to check gauge.

Pattern Notes

This shawl is worked from the top down with increases at each end and at the center point.

To make it easier to find where to work last stitch in each row of mesh pattern, place a stitch marker in 2nd chain of beginning chain-4.

If you want a smaller shawl (approximately 24½ inches long at center point with border), make 49 rows in the mesh pattern, then work the border decreasing the number of pattern repeats as necessary.

Weave in ends as work progresses.

Chain-4 at beginning of row counts as first half double crochet and chain-2 unless otherwise stated.

Chain-3 at beginning of row counts as first half double crochet and chain-1 unless otherwise stated.

Join with slip stitch as indicated unless otherwise stated.

Special Stitches

Shell: (2 dc, ch 1, 2 dc) in indicated place.

Fan: 11 tr in indicated place.

Large shell: (2 dc, ch 1, dc, ch 1, 2 dc) in indicated place.

Shawl

Mesh Body

Row 1 (RS): Beg at top with brilliant blues, ch 5, ({sc, ch 2} twice, hdc) in 5th ch from hook *(beg 4 sk chs count as an hdc and ch-2 sp)*, turn. Place marker in 2nd ch-2 sp. *(2 hdc, 2 sc, 3 ch-2 sps)*

Row 2: Ch 4 *(see Pattern Notes)*, sc in next ch-2 sp, (sc, ch 2, sc) in marked sp, move marker to ch-2 sp just made, ch 2, sc in next ch-2 sp, ch 2, hdc in 2nd ch of beg ch-4, turn. *(2 hdc, 4 sc, 5 ch-2 sps)*

Row 3: Ch 4, [sc in next ch-2 sp, ch 2] twice, (sc, ch 2, sc) in marked sp, move marker to ch-2 sp just made, [ch 2, sc in next ch-2 sp] twice, ch 2, hdc in 2nd ch of beg ch-4, turn. *(2 hdc, 6 sc, 7 ch-2 sps)*

Row 4: Ch 4, *sc in next ch-2 sp, ch 2, rep from * across to marked sp, (sc, ch 2, sc) in marked sp, move marker to ch-2 sp just made, **ch 2, sc in next ch-2 sp, rep from ** across to last ch-2 sp, ch 2, sc in last ch-2 sp, ch 2, hdc in 2nd ch of beg ch-4, turn. *(2 hdc, 8 sc, 9 ch-2 sps)*

Rows 5–84: Rep row 4. *(2 hdc, 168 sc, 169 ch-2 sps at end of last row)*

Border

Row 1: Ch 3 *(see Pattern Notes)*, sc in same st, [2 sc in next ch-2 sp, sc in next st] 84 times, (sc, ch 2, sc) in marked ch-2 sp, move stitch marker to ch-2 sp just made, [sc in next st, 2 sc in next ch-2 sp] 84 times, (sc, ch 1, hdc) in 2nd ch of beg ch-4, turn. *(2 hdc, 508 sc, 1 ch-2 sp, 2 ch-1 sps)*

Row 2: Ch 3 *(does not count as a st)*, dc in first st, sk next sc, **shell** *(see Special Stitches)* in next sc, ch 2, sk next 4 sc, sc in next sc, ch 4, sk next 4 sc, sc in next sc, ch 2**, sk next 4 sc, rep from * 17 times, ending last rep at **, sk next 2 sc, shell in marked ch-2 sp, remove marker, ch 2, sk next 2 sc, sc in next sc, ch 4, sk next 4 sc, sc in next sc, ch 2, sk next 4 sc, [shell in next sc, ch 2, sk next 4 sc, sc in next sc, ch 4, sk next 4 sc, sc in next sc, ch 2, sk next 4 sc] 16 times, shell next sc, sk next sc, dc in 2nd ch of beg ch-3, turn. *(35 shells, 2 dc, 68 sc, 34 ch-4 sps, 68 ch-2 sps)*

Row 3: Ch 3, dc in first st, ch 1, *shell in ch-1 sp of next shell, sk next ch-2 sp, **fan** *(see Special Stitches)* in next ch-4 sp, sk next ch-2 sp, rep from * 33 times, shell in next ch-1 sp, ch 1, sk next 2 sts, dc in last st, turn. *(35 shells, 34 fans, 2 dc, 2 ch-1 sps)*

Row 4: Ch 3, dc in first st, ch 2, *shell in ch-1 sp of next shell, ch 2, sk next 2 dc, sc in next tr, [ch 3, sk next tr, sc in next tr] 5 times, ch 2, rep from * 33 times, shell in ch-1 sp of next shell, ch 2, sk next 2 dc, dc in last st, turn. *(35 shells, 2 dc, 204 sc, 170 ch-3 sps, 70 ch-2 sps)*

Row 5: Ch 3, dc in first st, ch 3, *shell in ch-1 sp of next shell, ch 3, sk next ch-2 sp, sc in next ch-3 sp, [ch 3, sc in next ch-3 sp] 4 times, ch 3, rep from * 33 times, shell in ch-1 sp of next shell, ch 3, sk next ch-2 sp, dc in last st, turn. *(35 shells, 2 dc, 170 sc, 206 ch-3 sps)*

Row 6: Ch 3, dc in first st, ch 4, *shell in ch-1 sp of next shell, ch 4, sk next ch-3 sp, sc in next ch-3 sp, [ch 3, sc in next ch-3 sp] 3 times**, ch 4, rep from * 16 times, ending last rep at **, ch 5, shell in ch-1 sp of next shell, ch 5, sk next ch-3 sp, sc in next ch-3 sp, [ch

3, sc in next ch-3 sp] 3 times, ch 4, ***shell in ch-1 sp of next shell, ch 4, sk next ch-3 sp, sc in next ch-3 sp, [ch 3, sk next st, sc in next ch-3 sp] 3 times, ch 4, rep from *** 15 times, shell in ch-1 sp of next shell, ch 4, sk next ch-3 sp, dc in last st, turn. *(35 shells, 2 dc, 136 sc, 2 ch-5 sps, 68 ch-4 sps, 102 ch-3 sps)*

Row 7: Ch 3, dc in first st, ch 5, *shell in ch-1 sp of next shell, ch 5, sk next ch-4 sp, sc in next ch-3 sp, [ch 3, sc in next ch-3 sp] twice**, ch 5, rep from * 16 times, ending last rep at **, ch 6, shell in ch-1 sp of next shell, ch 6, sk next ch-5 sp, sc in next ch-3 sp, [ch 3, sc in next ch-3 sp] twice, ch 5, ***shell in ch-1 sp of next shell, ch 5, sk next ch-4 sp, sc in next ch-3 sp, [ch 3, sc in next ch-3 sp] twice, ch 5, rep from *** 15 times, shell in ch-1 sp of next shell, ch 5, sk next ch-4 sp, dc in last st, turn. *(35 shells, 2 dc, 102 sc, 2 ch-6 sps, 170 ch-5 sps, 68 ch-3 sps)*

Row 8: Ch 3, dc in first st, ch 5, ***large shell** (see Special Stitches) in ch-1 sp of next shell, ch 5, sk next ch-5 sp, sc in next ch-3 sp, ch 3, sc in next ch-3 sp**, ch 5, rep from * 16 times, ending last rep at **, ch 7, large shell in ch-1 sp of next shell, ch 7, sc in next ch-3 sp, ch 3, sc in next ch-3 sp, ch 5, ***large shell in ch-1 sp of next shell, ch 5, sk next ch-5 sp, sc in next ch-3 sp, ch 3, sc in next ch-3 sp, ch 5, rep from *** 15 times, large shell in ch-1 sp of next shell, ch 5, sk next ch-5 sp, dc in last st, turn. *(35 large shells, 2 dc, 68 sc, 2 ch-7 sps, 68 ch-5 sps, 34 ch-3 sps)*

Row 9: Ch 3, dc in first st, ch 6, *shell in next ch-1 sp of next large shell, ch 1, sk next st, shell in next ch-1 sp, ch 6, sc in next ch-3 sp**, ch 6, sk next ch-5 sp, rep from * 16 times, ending last rep at **, ch 8, shell in next ch-1 sp of next large shell, ch 1, sk next st, shell in next ch-1 sp, ch 8, sc in next ch-3 sp, ch 6, ***shell in next ch-1 sp of next large shell, ch 1, sk next st, shell in next ch-1 sp, ch 6, sc in next ch-3 sp, ch 6, rep from *** 15 times, shell in next ch-1 sp of next large shell, ch 1, sk next st, shell in next ch-1 sp, ch 6, sk next ch-5 sp, dc in last st, turn. *(70 shells, 2 dc, 34 sc, 68 ch-6 sps, 2 ch-8 sps, 35 ch-1 sps)*

Row 10: Ch 1, sk first st, *6 sc in next ch-6 sp, ch 3, sc in next ch-1 sp, ch 3, (sc, ch 3, sc) in next ch-1 sp, ch 3, sc in next ch-1 sp, ch 3, 6 sc in next ch-6 sp, rep from * 16 times, 8 sc in next ch-8 sp, ch 3, sc in next ch-1 sp, ch 3, (sc, ch 3, sc) in next ch-1 sp, ch 3, sc in next ch-1 sp, ch 3, 8 sc in next ch-8 sp, **6 sc in next ch-6 sp, ch 3, sc in next ch-1 sp, ch 3, (sc, ch 3, sc) in next ch-1 sp, ch 3, sc in next ch-1 sp, ch 3, 6 sc in next ch-6 sp, rep from ** 16 times, ch 1, sl st in last st. Fasten off. *(564 sc, 175 ch-3 sps)*

Finishing

For best results, wire block to open up mesh pattern fully. ●

Autumn Days Shawlette

Skill Level
■■■□□ EASY

Finished Measurements
58½ inches wide across top edge x 24½ inches long from top to bottom point

Materials

- Red Heart Boutique Unforgettable medium (worsted) weight acrylic yarn (3½ oz/270 yds/100g per ball):
  - 3 balls #3956 polo
- Size J/10/6mm crochet hook or size needed to obtain gauge
- Tapestry needle
- Stitch markers

Gauge
In pattern: 8 sc and 7 ch-2 sps = 4 inches; 17 rows = 4 inches

Take time to check gauge.

Pattern Notes
Shawl is worked from the top down with increases at each end and at center point.

To make it easier to find where to work last stitch in each row of mesh pattern, place a stitch marker in 2nd chain of beginning chain-4.

If a larger shawl (approximately 38 inches long at center point with border) is desired, work 111 rows in the mesh pattern, then work the border increasing the number of pattern repeats as necessary.

Chain-4 at beginning of row counts as first half double crochet and chain-2 space unless otherwise stated.

Special Stitches
Beginning fan (beg fan): Ch 4 *(see Pattern Notes)*, ({dc, ch 1} twice, dc) in indicated place.

Fan: ({Dc, ch 1} 5 times, dc) in indicated place.

Ending fan: [Dc, ch 1] 3 times in last ch-2 sp, dc in 2nd ch of beg ch.

V-stitch (V-st): (Dc, ch 1, dc) in indicated place.

Shawl

Mesh Body
Row 1 (RS): Beg at top, ch 5, ({sc, ch 2} twice, hdc) in 5th ch from hook *(beg 4 sk chs count as hdc and ch-2 sp)*, turn. Place marker in 2nd ch-2 sp. *(2 hdc, 2 sc, 3 ch-2 sps)*

Row 2: Ch 4 *(see Pattern Notes)*, sc in next ch-2 sp, ch 2, (sc, ch 2, sc) in marked sp, move marker to ch-2 sp just made, ch 2, sc in next ch-2 sp, ch 2, hdc in 2nd ch of beg ch-4, turn. *(2 hdc, 4 sc, 5 ch-2 sps)*

Row 3: Ch 4, [sc in next ch-2 sp, ch 2] twice, (sc, ch 2, sc) in marked sp, move marker to ch-2 sp just made, [ch 2, sc in next ch-2 sp] twice, ch 2, hdc in 2nd ch of beg ch-4, turn. *(2 hdc, 6 sc, 7 ch-2 sps)*

Row 4: Ch 4, *sc in next ch-2 sp, ch 2, rep from * across to marked sp, (sc, ch 2, sc) in marked sp, move marker to ch-2 sp just made, **ch 2, sc in next ch-2 sp, rep from ** across to last ch-2 sp, ch 2, sc in last ch-2 sp, ch 2, hdc in 2nd ch of beg ch-4, turn. *(2 hdc, 8 sc, 9 ch-2 sps)*

Rows 5–69: Rep row 4. *(2 hdc, 138 sc, 139 ch-2 sps at end of last row)*

Border
Row 1: Sk first st, **beg fan** *(see Special Stitches)* in first ch-2 sp, *sk next sc, sc in next sc, sk next sc, **fan** *(see Special Stitches)* in next ch-2 sp, rep from * 42 times,

sk next sc, sc in next sc, sk next sc, **ending fan** (see Special Stitches), turn. (45 fans, 44 sc)

Move marker to center ch-1 sp of fan made in marked ch-2 sp.

Row 2: Ch 4, sk first st, sc in next ch-1 sp, ch 2, sc in next ch-1 sp, ch 2, sk next 2 dc, [**V-st** (see Special Stitches) in next sc, ch 2, sk next 2 ch-1 sps, sc in next ch-1 sp, ch 2] 21 times, V-st in next sc, ch 2, sk next 2 dc, sc in next ch-1 sp, ch 2, sk next dc, (sc, ch 2, sc) in marked ch-1 sp, move marker to ch-2 sp just made, ch 2, sk next dc, sc in next ch-1 sp, ch 2, sk next 2 dc, [V-st in next sc, ch 2, sk next 2 ch-1 sps, sc in next ch-1 sp, ch 2] 21 times, V-st in next sc, ch 2, sk next ch-1 sp, sc in next ch-1 sp, ch 2, sk next dc, sc in next ch-1 sp, ch 2, hdc in 2nd ch of beg ch-4, turn. (44 V-sts, 2 hdc, 50 sc, 95 ch-2 sps)

Row 3: Sk first st, beg fan in next ch-2 sp, sk next sc, [sc in next sc, fan in ch-1 sp of next V-st] 22 times, sc in next sc, sk next sc, fan in marked ch-2 sp, [sc in next sc, fan in ch-1 sp of next V-st] 22 times, sc in next sc, sk next sc, end fan, turn. (47 fans, 46 sc)

Row 4: Ch 3, sk first st, sc in next ch-1 sp, ch 2, sc in next ch-1 sp, ch 2, [V-st in next sc, ch 2, sk next 2 ch-1 sps, sc in next ch-1 sp, ch 2] 22 times, V-st in next sc, ch 2, sk next ch-1 sp, sc in next ch-1 sp, ch 2, (sc, ch 2, sc) in marked ch-1 sp, move marker to ch-2 sp just made, ch 2, sc in next ch-1 sp, ch 2, [V-st in next sc, ch 2, sk next 2 ch-1 sps, sc in next ch-1 sp, ch 2] 22 times, V-st in next sc, ch 2, sk next ch-1 sp, sc in next ch-1 sp, ch 2, sk next dc, sc in next ch-1 sp, ch 2, hdc in 2nd ch of beg ch-4, turn. (46 V-sts, 51 sc, 99 ch-2 sps)

Row 5: Sk first st, beg fan in next ch-2 sp, sk next sc, [sc in next sc, fan in ch-1 sp of next V-st] 23 times, sk next ch-2 sp, sc in next sc, fan in marked ch-2 sp, sk next sc, [sc in next sc, fan in ch-1 sp of next V-st] 23 times, sk next ch-2 sp, sc in next sc, sk next sc, end fan. Fasten off. (49 fans, 48 sc)

Finishing
For best results, wire block to open up mesh pattern fully. ●

Hint of Spring
Continued from page 4

next 11 sts, sc dec in last st and in end of same row, sc in end of same row, 2 sc in end of each of next 56 rows, sl st in top of last st of row 2 of Border, ch 2, sc in end of row 3 of Border, sl st in top of last st of row 3 of Border, ch 2, sc in ch-3 sp at end of row 4, ch 2, working across sts of row 4 of Border, sk next st, sl st in next st, (sc, ch 3, sc) in next st, [sk next st, 2 sc in next ch-1 sp] 3 times, *sk next st, sl st in next ch-1 sp, [sk next st, 2 sc in next ch-1 sp] twice, sk next st, (sc, ch 3, sc) in next ch-1 sp, [sk next st, 2 sc in next ch-1 sp] twice*, rep from * to * 17 times, sk next st, sl st in next ch-1 sp, [sk next st, 2 sc in next ch-1 sp] 3 times, sk next st, (sc, ch 3, sc) in next ch-1 sp, [sk next st, 2 sc in next ch-1 sp] 3 times, rep from * to * 20 times, sk next st, sl st in next ch-1 sp, [sk next st, 2 sc in next ch-1 sp] 3 times, sk next st, (sc, ch 3, sc) in next ch-1 sp, [sk next st, 2 sc in next ch-1 sp] 3 times, rep from * to * 18 times, sk next st, sl st in next ch-1 sp, [sk next st, 2 sc in next ch-1 sp] 3 times, sk next st, (sc, ch 3, sc) in next ch-1 sp, join in next st. Fasten off. (733 sc, 65 sl sts, 60 ch-3 sps, 5 ch-2 sps)

Finishing
For best results, block to open up mesh pattern fully. ●

Winterfall Ruana

Skill Level

 EASY

Finished Measurements

43 inches wide across shoulders x 22½ inches long from shoulder to bottom edge x 22½ inches long from shoulder to front bottom edge

Front Panels: 20 inches wide

Materials

- Premier Yarns Deborah Norville Alpaca Dance medium (worsted) weight acrylic/alpaca yarn (3½ oz/371 yds/100g per ball):
    5 balls color #0010 lake blue

- Size J/10/6mm crochet hook or size needed to obtain gauge
- Tapestry needle
- Stitch markers

Gauge

14 foundation sc and 6 rows = 4 inches

Gauge is not important for this project. Finished fabric is very stretchy.

Pattern Notes

Ruana is worked in 3 panels, and then rows are worked on the neck edges of fronts and center back. To create a wider ruana, add stitches to foundation row in multiples of 8 (adds 2 more shells) and adjust repeats in rows 1 and 2 accordingly. To lengthen fronts, add rows in increments of 2.

For Neck Edging, spacing between shells at Center Back Neck is shorter than spacing between shells for Back and Front Panels to allow for ease at Neck.

Chain-3 at beginning of row does not count as a stitch unless otherwise stated.

Join with slip stitch as indicated unless otherwise stated.

Special Stitches

First foundation single crochet (first foundation sc): Ch 2, insert hook in 2nd ch from hook, yo, pull up lp, yo, pull through 1 lp on hook *(see illustration A—ch-1 completed)*, yo, pull through both lps on hook *(see illustrations B and C—sc completed)*.

Next foundation single crochet (next foundation sc): [Insert hook in last ch-1 made *(see illustration A)*, yo, pull up lp, yo, pull through 1 lp on hook *(see illustration B—ch-1 completed)*, yo, pull through both lps on hook *(see illustrations C and D—sc completed)*] as indicated.

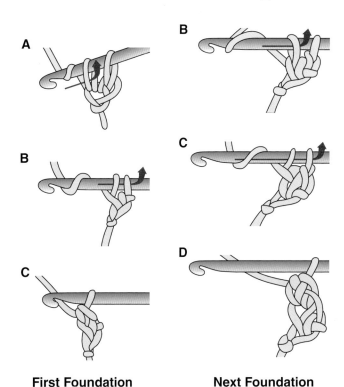

First Foundation Single Crochet

Next Foundation Single Crochet

Shell: (2 tr, ch 2, sc) in indicated place.

Edge shell: (Sc, dc, ch 2, sc) in indicated place.

Ruana

Back Panel
Foundation row: First foundation sc *(see Special Stitches)*, 132 **next foundation sc** *(see Special Stitches)*, turn. *(133 sts)*

Row 1(RS): Ch 3 *(see Pattern Notes)*, **shell** *(see Special Stitches)* in first st, [sk next 3 sts, shell in next st] 33 times, turn. *(34 shells)*

Row 2: Ch 3, shell in each ch-2 sp across, turn.

Rows 3–38: Rep row 2. At end of last row, fasten off.

Right Front Panel
Row 1 (RS): Hold Back Panel with RS facing and unworked side of foundation row at top, **join** *(see Pattern Notes)* in base of first foundation sc at right-hand edge, ch 3, shell in same st as beg ch-3, [sk next 3 sts, shell in next st] 15 times, leaving rem sts unworked, turn. *(16 shells)*

Row 2: Ch 1, **edge shell** *(see Special Stitches)* in first ch-2 sp, shell in ch-2 sp of each rem shell across, turn. *(15 shells, 1 edge shell)*

Row 3: Ch 3, shell in ch-2 sp of each shell across, turn. *(16 shells)*

Row 4: Ch 1, edge shell in first ch-2 sp, shell in ch-2 sp of each rem shell across, turn. *(15 shells, 1 edge shell)*

Rows 5–38: [Rep rows 3 and 4 alternately] 17 times. At end of last row, fasten off.

Left Front Panel
Row 1 (RS): With RS facing, sk next 11 sts on foundation row from Right Front Panel, join in next st, ch 1, edge shell in same st as beg ch-1, [sk next 3 sts, shell in next st] 15 times, turn. *(15 shells, 1 edge shell)*

Row 2: Ch 3, shell in each ch-2 sp across, turn. *(16 shells)*

Row 3: Ch 1, edge shell in first ch-2 sp, shell in each rem ch-2 sp across, turn. *(15 shells, 1 edge shell)*

Row 4: Ch 3, shell in each ch-2 sp across, turn. *(16 shells)*

Rows 5–38: [Rep rows 3 and 4 alternately] 17 times. At end of last row, do not fasten off.

Neck Edging
Row 1: Working across inside edge of Panel, ch 3, shell in side of first sc, [sk next row, shell in side of next sc] 18 times, sk next row, shell in foundation sc at base of last shell of foundation row, working across unworked sts of foundation row, [sk next 2 sts, shell in next st] 3 times, sk next 2 sts, working across side of Right Front Panel, shell in side of first sc, [sk next row, shell in side of next sc] 18 times, turn. *(42 shells)*

Row 2: Ch 3, shell in ch-2 sp of each of next 42 shells, turn. *(42 shells)*

Row 3: Ch 3, shell in each ch-2 sp across, turn.

Rows 4–9: Rep row 3. At end of last row, fasten off.

Finishing
Block gently as desired. ●

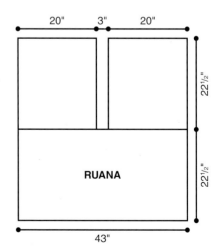

Frosty Mornings Crescent Shawl

Skill Level

 EASY

Finished Measurements

Approximately 75 inches wide x 16 inches long

Materials

- Premier Yarns Deborah Norville Alpaca Dance medium (worsted) weight acrylic/alpaca yarn (3½ oz/371 yds/100g per ball):
  3 balls #0016 silver fog
- Size J/10/6mm crochet hook or size needed to obtain gauge
- Tapestry needle
- Stitch markers

Gauge

In pattern: 6 V-sts = 5 inches; 8 rows = 5 inches

Gauge is not important for this project.

Pattern Notes

Weave in ends as work progresses.

Chain-3 at beginning of row does not count as a stitch unless otherwise stated.

Join with slip stitch as indicated unless otherwise stated.

Special Stitches

Increase V-stitch (inc V-st): ([Dc, ch 1] twice, dc) in indicated place.

V-stitch (V-st): (Dc, ch 1, dc) in indicated place.

Shell: (2 dc, ch 1, 2 dc) in indicated sp.

Fan: ([Dc, ch 1] 3 times, dc) in indicated sp.

V-stitch shell (V-st shell): V-st 3 times in indicated sp.

Shawl

Foundation row: Ch 2, sc in 2nd ch from hook, *ch 3, turn, dc in top of last sc, ch 1, turn, sc in top of last dc, rep from * 31 times. Do not turn. *(31 dc, 32 sc)*

Row 1: Working across side of foundation row, **ch 3** *(see Pattern Notes)*, (dc, **inc V-st**—*see Special Stitches*) in side of first sc, *sk next dc row, **V-st** *(see Special Stitches)* in side of next sc, rep from * 29 times, sk last dc row, (inc V-st, dc) in side of sc, turn. *(2 inc V-sts, 30 V-sts, 2 dc)*

Row 2: Ch 3, dc in first st, V-st in next ch-1 sp, V-st in next st, V-st next ch-1 sp, *V-st in ch-1 sp of next V-st, V-st in sp between V-sts, V-st in ch-1 sp of next V-st, rep from * 14 times, V-st in next ch-1 sp, V-st in next st, V-st in next ch-1 sp, sk next st, dc in last st, turn. *(51 V-sts, 2 dc)*

Row 3: Ch 3, dc in first st, sk next st, inc V-st in next ch-1 sp, V-st in ch-1 sp of each V-st across to last V-st, inc V-st in ch-1 sp of last V-st, sk next st, dc in last st, turn. *(2 inc V-sts, 49 V-sts, 2 dc)*

Row 4: Ch 3, dc in first st, V-st in next ch-1 sp, V-st in next st, V-st in next ch-1 sp, V-st in ch-1 sp of each V-st across to inc V-st, V-st in next ch-1 sp of inc V-st, V-st in next st, V-st in next ch-1 sp, sk next st, dc in last st, turn. *(55 V-sts, 2 dc)*

Row 5: Rep row 3. *(2 inc V-sts, 53 V-sts, 2 dc)*

Row 6: Rep row 4. *(59 V-sts, 2 dc)*

Row 7: Ch 3, dc in first st, inc V-st in next ch-1 sp, V-st in ch-1 sp of each of next 3 V-sts, *V-st in sp between V-sts, V-st in ch-1 sp of each of next 3 V-sts, rep from * 17 times, inc V-st in next ch-1 sp, sk next st, dc in last st, turn. *(2 inc V-sts, 75 V-sts, 2 dc)*

Row 8: Rep row 4. *(81 V-sts, 2 dc)*

Rows 9–16: [Rep rows 3 and 4 alternately] 4 times. *(97 V-sts, 2 dc at end of last row)*

Row 17: Ch 3, dc in first st, **shell** *(see Special Stitches)* in next ch-1 sp, [V-st in each of next 7 ch-1 sps, shell in next ch-1 sp] 12 times, sk next st, dc in last st, turn. *(13 shells, 84 V-sts, 2 dc)*

Row 18: Ch 3, dc in first st, shell in next ch-1 sp, [V-st in next ch-1 sp, shell in next ch-1 sp, V-st in each of next 3 ch-1 sps, shell in next ch-1 sp, V-st in next ch-1 sp, shell in next ch-1 sp] 12 times, sk next 2 sts, dc in last st, turn. *(37 shells, 60 V-sts, 2 dc)*

Row 19: Ch 3, dc in first st, shell in next ch-1 sp, [V-st in next ch-1 sp, shell in next ch-1 sp] 48 times, sk next 2 sts, dc in last st, turn. *(49 shells, 48 V-sts, 2 dc)*

Row 20: Ch 3, dc in first st, shell in next ch-1 sp, *shell in each of next 2 ch-1 sps, [V-st in next ch-1 sp, shell in next ch-1 sp] twice, shell in each of next 2 ch-1 sps, rep from * 11 times, sk next 2 sts, dc in last st, turn. *(73 shells, 24 V-sts, 2 dc)*

Row 21: Ch 3, dc in first st, shell in each ch-1 sp across, sk next 2 sts, dc in last st, turn. *(97 shells, 2 dc)*

Row 22: Ch 3, dc in first st, **fan** *(see Special Stitches)* in next ch-1 sp, [shell in each of next 3 ch-1 sps, fan in next ch-1 sp] 24 times, sk next 2 sts, dc in last st, turn. *(25 fans, 72 shells, 2 dc)*

Row 23: Ch 3, dc in first st, sk next ch-1 sp, fan in next ch-1 sp, [sk next ch-1 sp, shell in next ch-1 sp, fan in next ch-1 sp, shell in next ch-1 sp, sk next ch-1 sp, fan in next ch-1 sp] 24 times, sk next 2 sts, dc in last st, turn. *(49 fans, 48 shells, 2 dc)*

Row 24: Ch 3, dc in first st, sk next ch-1 sp, fan in next ch-1 sp, [fan in next ch-1 sp, sk next ch-1 sp, fan in next ch-1 sp] 48 times, sk next 2 sts, dc in last st, turn. *(97 fans, 2 dc)*

Row 25: Ch 3, dc in first st, sk next ch-1 sp, **V-st shell** *(see Special Stitches)* in next ch-1 sp, [sk next 2 ch-1 sps, fan in next ch-1 sp, sk next 2 ch-1 sps, V-st shell in next ch-1 sp] 48 times, sk next 2 sts, dc in last st, turn. *(48 fans, 49 V-st shells, 2 dc)*

Row 26: Ch 1, sl st in first st, sk next ch-1 sp, V-st shell in next ch-1 sp, [sk next 2 ch-1 sps, V-st shell in next ch-1 sp] 96 times, sk next 3 sts, sl st in last st, turn. *(97 V-st shells, 2 sl sts)*

Row 27: Ch 2, *sk next st, sc in next ch-1 sp, ch 3, sk next 2 sts, (sc, ch 2, sc) in next ch-1 sp, ch 3, sk next 2 sts, sc in next ch-1 sp**, sl st in sp between V-st shells, rep from * 96 times, ending last rep at **, ch 2, sl st in top of last dc in row 25. Fasten off. *(388 sc, 98 sl sts, 194 ch-3 sps, 99 ch-2 sps)*

Finishing
Block gently as desired. ●

Sassy Spring Wrap
Continued from page 6

Note: Rnd 1 is worked in both bottom and top of sts of foundation rnd).

Rnd 1 (RS): Ch 4 *(see Pattern Notes)*, (dc, ch 1, dc) in same st as beg ch-4 *(beg of first fan)*, *sk next 3 sts, sc in next st, ch 3, sc in next st, sk next 3 sts**, **fan** *(see Special Stitches)* in next st, rep from * 19 times, ending last rep at **, (dc, ch 1, dc, ch 1, dc) in same st as beg ch-4 *(first fan complete)*, join with sc in 3rd ch of beg ch-4, turn. *(20 fans, 40 sc, 40 ch-3 sps)*

Rnd 2: Ch 1, sc in sp formed by joining sc, *ch 2, sk next 2 ch-1 sps, **shell** *(see Special Stitches)* in next ch-3 sp, ch 2, sk next 2 ch-1 sps**, (sc, ch 3, sc) in next ch-1 sp, rep from * 19 times, ending last rep at **, sc in same sp as first sc made, ch 1, join with hdc in first sc of rnd *(counts as last ch-3 sp)*, turn. *(20 shells, 40 sc, 40 ch-2 sps, 20 ch-3 sps)*

Rnd 3: Ch 4, (dc, ch 1, dc) in next ch-1 sp, *sk next ch-2 sp, (sc, ch 3, sc) in next ch-3 sp, sk next ch-2 sp**, fan in next ch-3 sp, rep from * 19 times, ending last rep at **, (dc, ch 1, dc, ch 1, dc) in last ch-3 sp, join with sc in 3rd ch of beg ch-4, turn.

Rnds 4–7: [Rep rnds 2 and 3 alternately] twice. At end of last rnd, do not turn.

Rnd 8: Ch 1, (sc, ch 3, sc) in same sp as beg ch-1, *sc in next dc, in next ch-1 sp, and in next dc, **sc dec** *(see Stitch Guide)* in next ch-1 sp and in next ch-3 sp, ch 3, sc dec in same ch-3 sp and next ch-1 sp, sc in next dc, in next ch-1 sp and in next dc**, (sc, ch 3, sc) next ch-1 sp, rep from * 19 times, ending last rep at **, join in first sc. Fasten off. *(200 sc, 40 ch-3 sps)*

Finishing
Block gently as desired. ●

STITCH GUIDE

STITCH ABBREVIATIONS

beg	begin/begins/beginning
bpdc	back post double crochet
bpsc	back post single crochet
bptr	back post treble crochet
CC	contrasting color
ch(s)	chain(s)
ch-	refers to chain or space previously made (i.e., ch-1 space)
ch sp(s)	chain space(s)
cl(s)	cluster(s)
cm	centimeter(s)
dc	double crochet (singular/plural)
dc dec	double crochet 2 or more stitches together, as indicated
dec	decrease/decreases/decreasing
dtr	double treble crochet
ext	extended
fpdc	front post double crochet
fpsc	front post single crochet
fptr	front post treble crochet
g	gram(s)
hdc	half double crochet
hdc dec	half double crochet 2 or more stitches together, as indicated
inc	increase/increases/increasing
lp(s)	loop(s)
MC	main color
mm	millimeter(s)
oz	ounce(s)
pc	popcorn(s)
rem	remain/remains/remaining
rep(s)	repeat(s)
rnd(s)	round(s)
RS	right side
sc	single crochet (singular/plural)
sc dec	single crochet 2 or more stitches together, as indicated
sk	skip/skipped/skipping
sl st(s)	slip stitch(es)
sp(s)	space(s)/spaced
st(s)	stitch(es)
tog	together
tr	treble crochet
trtr	triple treble
WS	wrong side
yd(s)	yard(s)
yo	yarn over

YARN CONVERSION

OUNCES TO GRAMS	GRAMS TO OUNCES
1.............28.4	25................⅞
2.............56.7	40.............1⅔
3.............85.0	50.............1¾
4...........113.4	100...........3½

UNITED STATES		UNITED KINGDOM
sl st (slip stitch)	=	sc (single crochet)
sc (single crochet)	=	dc (double crochet)
hdc (half double crochet)	=	htr (half treble crochet)
dc (double crochet)	=	tr (treble crochet)
tr (treble crochet)	=	dtr (double treble crochet)
dtr (double treble crochet)	=	ttr (triple treble crochet)
skip	=	miss

Reverse single crochet (reverse sc): Ch 1, sk first st, working from left to right, insert hook in next st from front to back, draw up lp on hook, yo and draw through both lps on hook.

Chain (ch): Yo, pull through lp on hook.

Single crochet (sc): Insert hook in st, yo, pull through st, yo, pull through both lps on hook.

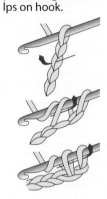

Double crochet (dc): Yo, insert hook in st, yo, pull through st, [yo, pull through 2 lps] twice.

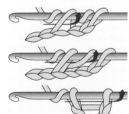

Front loop (front lp) Back loop (back lp)

Front Loop Back Loop

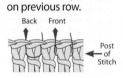

Front post stitch (fp): Back post stitch (bp): When working post st, insert hook from right to left around post of st on previous row.

Back   Front

Post of Stitch

Half double crochet (hdc): Yo, insert hook in st, yo, pull through st, yo, pull through all 3 lps on hook.

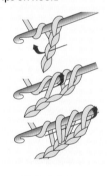

Double treble crochet (dtr): Yo 3 times, insert hook in st, yo, pull through st, [yo, pull through 2 lps] 4 times.

Slip stitch (sl st): Insert hook in st, pull through both lps on hook.

Chain color change (ch color change) Yo with new color, draw through last lp on hook.

Double crochet color change (dc color change) Drop first color, yo with new color, draw through last 2 lps of st.

Treble crochet (tr): Yo twice, insert hook in st, yo, pull through st, [yo, pull through 2 lps] 3 times.

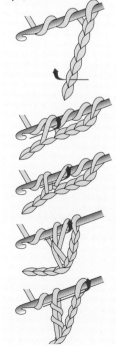

Single crochet decrease (sc dec): (Insert hook, yo, draw lp through) in each of the sts indicated, yo, draw through all lps on hook.

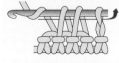

Example of 2-sc dec

Half double crochet decrease (hdc dec): (Yo, insert hook, yo, draw lp through) in each of the sts indicated, yo, draw through all lps on hook.

Example of 2-hdc dec

Double crochet decrease (dc dec): (Yo, insert hook, yo, draw lp through, yo, draw through 2 lps on hook) in each of the sts indicated, yo, draw through all lps on hook.

Example of 2-dc dec

Treble crochet decrease (tr dec): Holding back last lp of each st, tr in each of the sts indicated, yo, pull through all lps on hook.

Example of 2-tr dec

Metric Conversion Charts

METRIC CONVERSIONS

yards	x	.9144	=	metres (m)
yards	x	91.44	=	centimetres (cm)
inches	x	2.54	=	centimetres (cm)
inches	x	25.40	=	millimetres (mm)
inches	x	.0254	=	metres (m)

centimetres	x	.3937	=	inches
metres	x	1.0936	=	yards

INCHES INTO MILLIMETRES & CENTIMETRES (Rounded off slightly)

inches	mm	cm	inches	cm	inches	cm	inches	cm
1/8	3	0.3	5	12.5	21	53.5	38	96.5
1/4	6	0.6	5 1/2	14	22	56	39	99
3/8	10	1	6	15	23	58.5	40	101.5
1/2	13	1.3	7	18	24	61	41	104
5/8	15	1.5	8	20.5	25	63.5	42	106.5
3/4	20	2	9	23	26	66	43	109
7/8	22	2.2	10	25.5	27	68.5	44	112
1	25	2.5	11	28	28	71	45	114.5
1 1/4	32	3.2	12	30.5	29	73.5	46	117
1 1/2	38	3.8	13	33	30	76	47	119.5
1 3/4	45	4.5	14	35.5	31	79	48	122
2	50	5	15	38	32	81.5	49	124.5
2 1/2	65	6.5	16	40.5	33	84	50	127
3	75	7.5	17	43	34	86.5		
3 1/2	90	9	18	46	35	89		
4	100	10	19	48.5	36	91.5		
4 1/2	115	11.5	20	51	37	94		

KNITTING NEEDLES CONVERSION CHART

Canada/U.S.	0	1	2	3	4	5	6	7	8	9	10	10½	11	13	15
Metric (mm)	2	2¼	2¾	3¼	3½	3¾	4	4½	5	5½	6	6½	8	9	10

CROCHET HOOKS CONVERSION CHART

Canada/U.S.	1/B	2/C	3/D	4/E	5/F	6/G	8/H	9/I	10/J	10½/K	N
Metric (mm)	2.25	2.75	3.25	3.5	3.75	4.25	5	5.5	6	6.5	9.0

Annie's®

Wraps for All Seasons is published by Annie's, 306 East Parr Road, Berne, IN 46711. Printed in USA. Copyright © 2016 Annie's. All rights reserved. This publication may not be reproduced in part or in whole without written permission from the publisher.

RETAIL STORES: If you would like to carry this publication or any other Annie's publication, visit AnniesWSL.com.

Every effort has been made to ensure that the instructions in this publication are complete and accurate. We cannot, however, take responsibility for human error, typographical mistakes or variations in individual work. Please visit AnniesCustomerService.com to check for pattern updates.

ISBN: 978-1-59012-644-8

1 2 3 4 5 6 7 8 9